Perfect
NEW FOREST

MIKE READ

HALSGROVE

First published in Great Britain in 2008

Copyright © Mike Read 2008

British Library Cataloguing-in-Publication Data
A CIP record for this title is available from the British Library

ISBN 978 1 84114 756 7

HALSGROVE
Halsgrove House
Ryelands Industrial Estate
Bagley Road, Wellington, Somerset TA21 9PZ
Tel: 01823 653777   Fax: 01823 216796
email: sales@halsgrove.com
website: www.halsgrove.com

Printed and bound by
Grafiche Flaminia, Italy

INTRODUCTION

Since the setting up of the New Forest National Park Authority, the area can almost be described as being 'under new management'. However the opportunity now exists for this fresh tier of involvement to not only forward the positives that have come about over many centuries of 'management' but also to encourage a greater drive for environmental education as well as many other things. The visitors and locals really do need to know exactly what makes this area tick; what makes it the superb and unique area it has developed into.

Of course, every new initiative or planning, every new piece of thinking needs to incorporate the old ways of the Forest. Change for change's sake is not acceptable. But change that can further enhance the beauty, wildlife or character (or even the characters!) must be the way forward.

This photographic book aims to show in an artistic way some, but by no means all, of what is good and beautiful about the New Forest National Park. The wildlife content is kept to a minimum in these pages and will, perhaps, be the subject of a future title.

No matter what time of year or day you visit the New Forest, there is true beauty all around if only you have the eyes to look and the open mind to appreciate it. Of course, with the high speed living that many of us are now involved in, there is often little time to appreciate what is around us. All too often drivers ignore the 40 miles per hour limit as they speed off to or from work. At times we really do need to 'unhasten our lives' by allowing an extra few minutes to cross this area where ponies, cattle and deer often wander on to the roads. They, like the Forest's speed limit, should be incorporated into our thinking – every day. Take the time to drive that little more slowly, to appreciate the beauty everywhere and the Forest will be the kind of place you can begin to appreciate.

And the Forest really is a beautiful place. As some of the images in these pages show, by walking, peace and quiet can be found – and appreciated. Not only can you walk, stand or sit to contemplate this beauty but also at times the Forest will absorb your thinking. Then you will truly be able to reflect on its, and maybe your own, way of life.

Perhaps this book will inspire you to get out there and begin this appreciation and reflection or possibly you will see in the photographs enough to bring the Forest into your life without the need for you to actually be there. Or maybe certain images will enable you to remember a visit to a special place or moment in the Forest once you are at home, far from this lovely National Park. Enjoy.

An oak tree is bathed in a halo of mist as the sun peers over the trees beyond.
Back-lighting gives the picture an almost monochromatic look.

Walkers enjoy a stroll in the late summer sunshine on heathland near Long Slade Bottom. The scent of the blooming heather adds to the experience ... as does a refreshing pint in one of the Forest's local inns!

A Scots pine stands sentinel over heathland at Vales Moor as the sun sinks beneath the horizon to end yet another fine day.

As days lengthen in April, beech buds swell and leaves open on some of Britain's finest trees. At the same time, migrant birds arrive to join resident species in the woodlands and shortly after sunrise they sing to advertise their presence. It's almost as if they too are celebrating the uniqueness of the New Forest.

Low mist seems to be heralding the end of summer and greeting the beginning of autumn, a fabulous season of plenty in the Forest as trees, shrubs and flowering plants all produce seeds or fruit that birds and mammals can feed on.

Some of the ancient beech trees in the Forest are magnificent as here in Mark Ash Wood. However, in many locations, are there really enough younger trees coming on to replace the decaying and falling giants?

Afternoon sunshine filters through scattered conifers and lights up clumps of late-blooming heather.

This view across the Dockens Water Valley to Whitefield Plantation on Ibsley Common typifies the beauty of the Forest's open heathland on which so much rare and endangered wildlife relies.

Cycling is becoming an increasingly popular way of enjoying the beauty of the New Forest. These bikers are sticking to the approved routes but sadly many people ignore local by-laws and cycle wherever they wish, damaging fragile habitats.

Autumn is well and truly on the way as bracken turns a lovely shade of brown and soon the trees
in Digden Bottom will follow suit.

Four details noticed during a single winter walk. Have you the eyes to see, appreciate and enjoy such beauty?

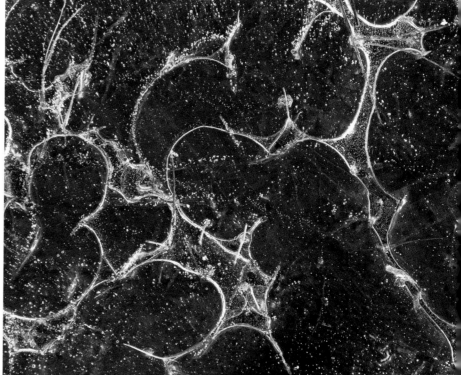

Sunlight penetrates the mist of a late autumn morning in the oak plantation in Broomy Inclosure.

This foal seems about to head off to explore on its own while mum feeds. Foals rarely wander off too far and mares can be very protective of their offspring.

The heart has rotted out of this oak tree yet the outer layers and the bark still convey enough nutrients to a much-reduced canopy for the tree to survive against all the odds.

Scots pines stand silhouetted against a deeply-coloured sunset. Soon the light will fade and another memorable day in the New Forest will pass and the night shift, such as owls and badgers, will emerge to begin their activities.

When fungi invades an ancient tree like this, it may take many years for it to reach a stage where the largest of branches break and fall. Soon, all of the nutrients held within this formerly magnificent specimen will be 'recycled' and aid other trees to grow.

With global warming now a recognised reality, more frequent storms cause scenes like this to become increasingly common.

The Rhinefield Ornamental Drive is well worth a visit when the rhododendrons are blooming. However, it is important for this introduced species to be controlled otherwise it will spread and choke out native plants which are more valuable to wildlife.

The gorgeous rolling heathlands of the New Forest are some of the most extensive heaths remaining intact in Europe, perhaps the world. Their importance, in conservation terms, cannot be underestimated. They look great too!

(Right) Holes in old beeches provide many birds with potential nest sites. The Forest still retains good populations of birds such as nuthatch, common redstart and various tit species.

(Left) The venue for the annual Boxing Day point-to-point changes from year to year and is a closely guarded secret until Christmas Day. That way, riders do not get the opportunity to research their possible route. It is the only true point-to-point remaining in Britain.

To wander among some of the Forest's ancient beech trees has been compared to entering a magnificent cathedral. Certainly standing beside some of these wonderful trees and speculating what history they have witnessed can be rather humbling.

Bracken, ling and a scattering of trees all add important elements to the composition of this heathland picture.

The blooming heather in the foreground indicates that this is a late summer picture. Here we enjoy a broad vista from Sandy Ridge across Backley Bottom to further heathland at Backley Holmes.

As Artist's Fungus (Ganoderma applanatum) rots this old pollarded beech tree, branches will soon be lost and eventually the whole plant will sadly die. I guess we should treasure every aspect of the Forest, and our own lives, before time runs out!

Bratley Wood hosts some fabulous trees but every visit, even to a familiar location, reveals something different.

High cirrus clouds mask the sun as frost cloaks the grassy heathland at Ober Corner.

Recent rains had increased the flow in the Ober Water stream to such an extent that at one place froth is forming on the surface. Here the bubbles seem trapped in an eddy and add an extra dimension to the scene.

Soon the sun will rise above the trees at the edge of Amberwood Inclosure and melt away the frost from the heathland nearby.

Oak trees stand proudly on Fritham Plain as the mist clears on a fine winter's day.

Larch trees grow tall and straight in plantations such as here in Puckpits Inclosure. These are part of the timber crop that helps contribute income to maintain this wonderful 'living Forest'.

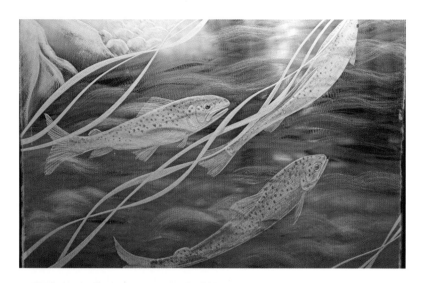

St John the Baptist church at Boldre is graced by a superbly engraved Millennium Window that reflects much of the local wildlife. The artist should be congratulated on the work and the church is well worth a visit for this feature alone!

Pub signs are an art form all of their own. Many names reflect an historical connection and the New Forest is rich in history depicted in this way. Visit the pubs to find out more or just to find refreshment and good food too.

The Solent and other parts of the New Forest coast form an important area for migrant, wintering and breeding birds. Here, as the sun rises over the Isle of Wight, Brent geese can be seen beside feeding ducks and waders.

Sowley Pond on the Beaulieu Estate can hold unusual birds especially during the winter months. Good views can be obtained from the road as this scene shows.

As the sun rises over a group of maturing Scots pines, its rays penetrate the light mist and soon the frost will be gone.

In many New Forest woodlands, the mature broad-leaved trees have an understory of holly. This combination provides an increased opportunity for birds to breed and feed.

Cattle rest beneath trees on Half Moon Common. When most people think of the New Forest, they think of the ponies and forget the importance of cattle in the area.

Lowland heath at Furzley Common from Stagbury Hill. This little-known corner of the New Forest is well worth exploring.

The picturesque Ashlett Quay on the Solent shoreline.

The salt marsh beside the Solent provides a winter home to hundreds of birds and in the summer months many will breed here. This area of Calshot Marshes is so important it is a designated Nature Reserve.

For many years New Forest streams were straightened to aid drainage which, in turn, helped trees to grow more quickly. Now, the wisdom of retaining water for conservation purposes (and to help avoid flooding) is more fully appreciated and the original water courses are being reinstated.

All Saints' church at Minstead on a beautiful spring day. This churchyard is the final resting place for Sir Arthur Conan Doyle, author of the Sherlock Holmes mysteries.

Ridges of heathland are bisected by trees in lower lying areas of Soarley Bottom. In the distance the pine plantation of Highland Water Inclosure can be made out through the mist.

In spring the ancient beech woods take on a new lease of life. Bird song fills the air amongst the fresh spring green leaves as the days lengthen and warm in the sunshine.

Some of the old, pollarded beech trees on Vinney Ridge are truly magnificent.

A spider's web in autumnal
beech branches is enhanced
with droplets of moisture
deposited during a misty night.

New Forest ponies are gathered annually in 'drifts'. A group of ponies is driven towards a pound close to Brockenhurst.
It certainly pays not to get in the way as pony hooves can be very painful and some of the riders have sharp tongues!

Some drifts will bring in large groups of ponies and they sometimes have to cross roads to reach the pound (holding pen). Traffic is usually held back as the herd approaches the road.

Two Commoners, who own some of these ponies, comment to each other about who owns which mare or foal.

Ponies have their tails clipped in various ways to denote on which part of the Forest their owners live.

Many of the ponies are released back on to the Forest at the end of a drift while others may be taken off for selling or holding on the Commoners own land.

A foal in the ring at Beaulieu Road pony sales. It will soon be in the hands of new owners.

Evening sunlight picks out the blooming heather while the trees of Soarley Beeches add a typical New Forest backdrop.

July and August see the best of the heather blossom in the New Forest.

Viewed from Castle Hill near Burley, mist lies low across Cranes Moor National Nature Reserve on the western edge of the Forest. Bournemouth and the Purbeck Hills can be seen in the distance.

To the right of the heathland lies Stinking Edge Wood (perhaps named for the slightly malodorous bog nearby!) while beyond are the conifers of North Oakley Inclosure at Blackensford Hill.

A mare and her young foal wander the heath of Ragged Boys Hill. Much of what the foal learns (where to eat, drink and shelter) will be inherited from its mother.

(Left) As we head towards autumn, the heather has just about finished blooming and the bracken has begun to take on a golden glow in this gloriously lit sunrise.

The mists of autumn envelop this double-trunked Scots pine as the sun peers through the gloom. Soon the mist will clear to reveal another superb day for exploring this beautiful National Park.

Often referred to as 'Lady of the Woods', silver birches add grace to a scene even when they grow on open heathland such as here at Ober Heath.

Dawn breaks over what remains of a timber plantation. A few trees still stand tall but soon newly planted conifers will crowd the area with dense green foliage and the cycle will begin again.

The colour of the sky deepens as the sun disappears over the distant horizon and mist begins to form in the valley below Picket Post.

The view from Rockford Common to Ibsley Common shows vast areas of lowland heath, a rare habitat in world terms.

During a drift a lone rider waits to head off any ponies heading away from the pound.

A group of ponies instinctively avoid the boggier parts and gallop across the safer heathland edge during a drift.

Reflections in the Highland Water stream add depth and colour to the scene.

The sun has risen quite high and a little mist remains to help cast beams of light through the branches of this magnificent pollarded beech.

A small group of Scots pines stand beside the track that leads through areas of heathland and down towards Burley Old House.

Autumn colours at their best beside the Linwood Road at Moyles Court.

A quieter moment along the Bolderwood Ornamental Drive. Many people come to savour the autumn colours along this stretch of minor road and it can be fairly busy at times …

… but take a stroll into Mark Ash Wood and you will easily find peace and quiet as well as some fabulous trees.

The sun rises above Rockford Common and soon the beautiful frost will be gone.

Above Foulford Bottom heathland sweeps up towards the A31 at Picket Post while the dry, brown bracken adds a warmer tone to this winter scene.

The Blackwater Arboretum off the Rhinefield Ornamental Drive holds a wide range of tree species from around the world. In autumn the colours can be quite spectacular. Take a closer look.

Blue Atlas Cedar foliage.

Sweet Gum leaves.

Fallen Japanese Cherry leaves.

Cappadocian Maple leaf.

Some of the Forest's cottages are even older than this 1876 property.

Many of the New Forest's wetlands are home to rare and declining wildlife such as dragonflies and damselflies. Some mires were drained in the past but now they are being re-instated.

Taken just a few minutes apart, these two pictures of the same tree show how changing the camera's position can make a big difference to the atmosphere of a location.

Are these straight trunks destined for timber production or are they there for future generations to enjoy for centuries to come?

Frost on Hincheslea Moor near Brockenhurst; a beautiful and transient moment captured by the camera.

Light rays break through a stand of Scots pines and bring life to the scene. Purple moor grass shows that the foreground soil is permanently wet so beware where you walk!

A glorious sunrise lights up the clouds and the pines growing near Horseshoe Bottom. Later the cloud cover increased and by lunchtime it was raining. Enjoy and treasure every moment of good weather, it may soon change!

The location may be called Hincheslea 'Moor' but this is true heathland, a rare habitat often full of endangered wildlife.

Oaks and distant Scots pines are silhouetted against a glorious, clear-sky sunset.

The Lin Brook stream at Greenford Bottom. As often happens in the lower lying parts of the New Forest, frost forms and covers the ground in the early morning.

This pathway and footbridge provide a safe passage across the Soldiers Bog to the north of Burley.
Some of the Forest's bogs are really treacherous!

Timber lies stacked beside a Forest road awaiting collection in Roe Inclosure. While we like to think of this National Park purely as a recreational and conservation area, it has to be remembered that this is a working forest.

A traditional type of view with much of the scene framed by the arching oak branch.

Wild daffodils are rare in the New Forest. This superb scene brightens a spring day ... if you know where to look.

Recent rains have soaked the woodland floor and this rivulet leads the eye nicely into this winter scene.

Look closely at this multi-trunked birch and the shapes of the old ivy stems add an intricate pattern to the picture.

Some areas of heather are cut each year. The resulting bales can be used in wet areas as submerged dams as the heather stems do not rot. It also stimulates a new flush of heather growth and is a good conservation measure.

The new logo for the New Forest National Park denotes the boundary on most approach roads
as here on a snowy April day in 2008.

Snow, a rarity in the New Forest, clings to the trunks of a row of birch trees following a spell of unseasonal weather.

At Linwood this road winds its way through oaks and other trees cloaked with a fresh fall of snow.
Are winters like this really a thing of the past?

A pony shelters from a cooling breeze in the lee of a group of snow-covered gorse bushes.

Even with snow all around, ponies still need to drink.
This trough near Fritham has attracted a passing group that pause to quench their thirst.

Eyeworth Pond at Fritham attracts many people who visit to feed the ducks. Amongst the wildfowl can be seen a number of Mandarin Ducks which are now very rare in their native China.

Blue sky and sunshine herald a thaw after this springtime snowfall. This scene was taken from the car park at Mogshade Hill towards Bratley Inclosure and Bratley Wood.

The White Swan public house overlooks Swan Green close to Lyndhurst, as do a few beautiful, often-photographed thatched cottages.

Beehive Cottage overlooks Swan Green.

A group of cattle stands close to fields at Fritham.

Malcolm Horsburgh and Shaun Bowles head across Hampton Ridge towards the Royal Oak at Fritham. Can you be breathalised on Forest tracks while driving a pony and trap?!

Sun peers round an aged beech tree to herald another spring day in the New Forest.

Three grey ponies graze their way up a heathery slope near Godshill.
Through the line of trees beyond, grassy fields can be seen.

The late Sir Dudley Forwood, the Official Verderer for eight years, is remembered close to his former Burley Old House home. The two oak trees were planted in Sir Dudley's memory.

Giant Redwood trees grow beside the Rhinefield Ornamental Drive. A place to sit a while and enjoy the beauty of some magnificent trees?

The Blackwater stream runs close to the major car park in the Rhinefield Ornamental Drive.

Heathland close to Burley, like most of the Forest's heather-clad open areas, is home to a variety of rare wildlife including types of lizards, snakes and birds.

Oaks reflected in a New Forest stream. Spring, as shown here, is a superb time to visit an oak wood when many birds will be singing. In autumn, deer will feed on fallen acorns.

Sunlight catches the trunk of a tree which is growing among a carpet of ramsons or wild garlic.

Soon, a thin veil of mist rises and rays of sunlight illuminate the delicate white blossoms.

Ponies stand beside the Ober Water stream close to Ober Corner.

Is this pony really checking the water temperature before crossing?

In a few places a carpet of bluebells grows beneath the cover of beech trees. Perhaps the acid soils of the Forest do not suit them too well but they still need to bloom and set seed before the leaf canopy closes out most of the light.

These bluebells are in Broomy Inclosure.

Wood spurge is an indicator plant of ancient woodland: consequently it can be found in many New Forest locations.

The autumn drifts (when New Forest Ponies are gathered for health checks, marking and for sale) take place at high speed even along Forest roads. Be aware of ponies on roads at any season.

Foals follow their mother's example and, as soon as they can, they will walk, trot or even gallop to keep up.

Mares and foals gather on grassland near White Moor in beautiful evening light. As they grow older, foals may be seen dashing about as they test and strengthen their legs.

A well grown foal still sticks close to its mother as the photographer appears out of the autumnal mist!

This foal may still suckle occasionally when its mother allows but it is now mostly reliant on grazing and browsing for its nutrition.

As we head deep into autumn and towards the short days of winter, grass grows less well, so many ponies will be found in the woods where other foods are perhaps available.

A couple of grey ponies on heathland at Digden Bottom with Whitefield Plantation beyond. Autumn has well and truly set in.

A couple of fallow deer bucks seen on a roadside. In autumn, male deer wander widely in search of mates so it is the best season to encounter them.

If you are either cautious or very lucky, it is sometimes possible to get really close to deer.

Well into November, fallow bucks may still associate with groups of does in case one comes into season but most will be mated during the rut in October.

Crossing the finish line at the 2007 Boxing Day point-to-point at Spy Holms near Burley.

Following a wet night, temperatures fell as the sky cleared just before dawn. These ponies were warming up
and drying out in the early sunshine.

Ponies know where the best water is to be found and will sometimes walk a considerable distance to their preferred water source.

Gorse and holly provide ponies with lots of nutrients during the winter months especially when lower temperatures and short days mean that the grass will grow more slowly.

You scratch my back and I'll scratch yours! Is mutual grooming really about curing an itch or does it help to establish 'friendships' between individual animals?

Grazing as the sun sets over Backley Plain to end another beautiful New Forest day.